Jean Fanchette
Equinox Island
Poems 1954–1991

Translated from the French by Hassan Melehy

Afterwords by Michel Deguy and J. M. G. Le Clézio

SPUYTEN DUYVIL

New York City

© 2025 by Hassan Melehy
ISBN 978-1-963908-84-8

Library of Congress Control Number: 2025942599

TABLE OF CONTENTS

EQUINOX ISLAND

Translator's Introduction

William S. Burroughs, Michel Deguy, Yves Bonnefoy, Allen Ginsberg, Octavio Paz, Anaïs Nin, Lawrence Durrell, Henry Miller: these are names well known in Euro-American literature, authors who spent time in Paris in the years after, and in some cases the years before, the Second World War. Here's another name: Jean Fanchette. Though he had ties to them all, he's well known only in some circles, especially the literary scenes of his native Mauritius and the other Indian Ocean islands of Rodrigues, Réunion, Madagascar, the Comoros, and Seychelles, where the most prestigious literary prize bears his name. For more than twenty years, the jury for the Prix Jean Fanchette has been led by 2008 Nobel laureate J. M. G. Le Clézio, a Mauritian by heritage.

Interest in Fanchette's work has grown: in June 2016, Columbia University's Reid Hall in Paris hosted a one-day conference devoted to his three vocations, poetry, publishing, and psychiatry (he was a medical doctor and made important contributions to the field). Timed with this event was the release of the third edition of *L'Île Équinoxe*: including poems from the collections he published in his lifetime and a selection of others, this book first appeared in 1993 (Éditions Stock), the year following his untimely death on March 29, 1992, at age fifty-nine. The 2016 edition is a reprint of the 2009 edition (Éditions Philippe Rey), with a preface by Le Clézio and a postface by Deguy (which served as the preface to the 1993 edition); my translations of these essays are the afterwords to this volume. The fourth edition appeared in 2023.

Born in Rose Hill, Mauritius, on May 6, 1932, Jean Fanchette left home at nineteen to study medicine on a *bourse d'Angleterre*, a scholarship granted by the British Empire to exceptional students in the colonies; he made special arrangements to pursue his studies in Paris, also envisioning a writing career. He spent his adult life in Paris, becoming a French citizen in 1970, and raising three daughters, Frédérique, Sylvie, and Véronique, with his wife Martine, a painter. In the Anglophone world he's best known as an editor and publisher: in 1959, with the support of Anaïs Nin, he founded the bilingual review *Two Cities*, which appeared until 1964. The other city of the Dickens-inspired title was ambiguously London and New York, signaling a transatlantic network of experimental writing that spanned from the Surrealists to the Beat Generation. This journal featured the work of many emerging notables, including those I named at the start of this introduction. Under the Two Cities imprint, he published *Minutes to Go* (1959), the "cut-ups" by William Burroughs, Brion Gysin, Sinclair Beiles, and Gregory Corso, who were then living in a low-grade Latin Quarter hotel; many regard this little book as a milestone in experimental literature. Fanchette was also honored for his own writing: in 1956 he won the Prix Paul Valéry and in 1958 the Prix Fénéon, both while he was still a medical student. His 1975 novel *Alpha du Centaure* (*Alpha Centauri*) won the Prix de la Langue Française from the Académie Française. He won the Prix des Mascareignes (Mascarene Islands Prize) for his 1971 study *Psychodrame et Théâtre moderne* (*Psychodrama and Modern Theater*). In 1977, he relaunched Two Cities Editions, issuing numerous books in French and English, mostly literary and some on psychiatry. At the time of his death he left two books unfinished, a psychiatric study and a novel.

Two Cities featured Francophone and Anglophone writings equally, a reflection of the suspicion of national borders held by many writers following the horrors of the Second World War and in the barricaded societies of the Cold War. French and English were also the two major imperial languages of the time, and hence the two metropolitan languages of Fanchette's upbringing and education: though Mauritius was part of the British Empire from 1810 until independence in 1968, nearly a century of prior French rule had left its linguistic imprint. This bilingualism of late colonial and postcolonial experience punctuates Fanchette's poetry. And it has everything to do with the cosmopolitanism of his writing and his work as editor and publisher, all of which travels along lesser-known paths linking regions and continents.

Something Fanchette shared with some of the writers he published is exile. A theme running through his poetry as well as *Alpha du Centaure* is exile from his native Mauritius; even the title *L'Île Équinoxe* contains the word *exil* in anagram. Mauritius, an island at the crossroads of Africa and the Indian subcontinent, was always a place he expressed longing for but also contentment at having left. As was the case for Gregory Corso and Allen Ginsberg, the Paris that Fanchette fulfilled his dream of coming to was the home of poets of near-mythical stature—Charles Baudelaire, Arthur Rimbaud, Paul Verlaine, Guillaume Apollinaire.

As Fanchette formed his poetic expression in the 1950s, in imagery, thematics, and structure his writing shows an affinity for Rimbaud and Verlaine as well as their literary descendants the Surrealists; he acknowledges a debt to one of the most capacious movements in global Francophone poetry, Negritude. Until the early 1960s, Fanchette often worked in lapidary formalism reminiscent of Baudelaire, also reflecting an immersion (like Baudelaire) in the long tradition of French poetry going back to the sixteenth century. His work shows no shortage of free verse, prose poetry, or experimentation. Filled with murmurs, shadowy landscapes, and seaside expanses, his poems grasp at receding memories through sensory detail, evoking multiple and conflicting truths. His attention to natural phenomena—water, trees, wind, animals, landscapes—and his preoccupation with exile bring him into contact with Saint-John Perse, a poet from another archipelago under colonial rule. Through allusion, Fanchette reveals his intimacy with an array of poetic currents in several languages.

Especially in a book of translated poetry, it's hardly worth revisiting the countless pronouncements on the obstacles to translating poetry. Whether it's French poet and theorist Joachim Du Bellay noting in

1549 that translation can't capture "that Energy and elusive Spirit" or linguist Roman Jakobson in 1959 flatly stating that poetry "by definition is untranslatable," it's obvious that none of this has ever kept translators from tackling poetry. It's also obvious that the tight intertwining of form and sense in poetry makes its translation, far more than that of prose, an approximation, even an analogy. The best a translator can convey is what the original poetry reads, looks, sounds, and feels like, often in pursuit of a method as vague as this formulation.

My biggest challenge in translating L'Île Équinoxe was Fanchette's formal verse. Is it even possible to carry a poem in meter and rhyme over to different metrical conventions and different word structure from those of the original language? Though I admire those English versions of Baudelaire that precisely transpose his alexandrines and decasyllables into iambic pentameter (a correspondence that has existed since the sixteenth century) and signal the meaning of the French, they fall short of illustrating the macabre mysteries seeping through the words of Les Fleurs du mal. Trying to avoid comparable thinning, I took license, relying on slant rhymes and the wiggle room built into anglophone meter. I also resorted to rhymed free verse, firmly implanted in anglophone poetry by a poet Fanchette obviously admired, T. S. Eliot.

Fanchette's open form verse and prose poems took me less time. They still demanded that I gauge his tone and mood, offer an idea of his paces, rhythms, and phonetics, and find words and phrases that suggest the concentrated, multidirectional senses of his. Sometimes, thanks to the interwoven histories of French and English, equivalents appeared on my page with little coaxing.

———————

Like all books, this one is the result of team effort. My warmest thanks go to my life partner and soulmate Dorothea Heitsch, who scrutinized every letter of my translation alongside Fanchette's original with her dazzling multilingualism. I'm grateful to Véronique Fanchette for her enthusiastic support from the moment I began this project; to Philippe Rey for publishing *L'Île Équinoxe* in the first place and wishing to see it translated; to Marie-Armelle Deguy and J. M. G. Le Clézio for their support of the project. And to John McLeod for his generous advice at key steps. And I thank my editor at Spuyten Duyvil, Aurelia Lavallee, for the personable professionalism that has made publishing this book a pleasure from submission through print. Also at Spuyten Duyvil, thanks to TT for doing such a fabulous job with typesetting and cover design.

Hassan Melehy
Chapel Hill, North Carolina, USA

EQUINOX ISLAND
POEMS 1954–1991

to Martine

How Shall I Say It?

I've always written poems. Poetry has been the testimony to my most constant fidelity to the unsayable, an unconscious and ferocious struggle, and at the same time a destination rather than a destiny.

Long after I awkwardly drafted my first poem, personal analysis and psychoanalytic praxis taught me what had moved, what was effected behind the writing. Moreover, I composed most of the poems in *The Visitation of the Plover Bird*, dedicated as they should be to René Major, in that state of dispossession-reverie or clairvoyance, as it were, that sometimes follows a session of psychoanalysis.

I've chosen to collect certain poems here that I've written, whether published or not, that have taught me to *read* myself.

The back country of these poems is naturally the island of my childhood: Mauritius, its salvos that won't stop reverberating in the echoes of exile, those deaf blazes in memory.

My debt to a few is obvious. To Robert Ganzo; to Yves Bonnefoy, who was a close and thoughtful friend over these...hidden years. To Lawrence Durrell, who taught me freedom. I should here add the name of Jean Paulhan, who gave to the very young man I was proof of his confidence, and that of René Char, the friend I never met who, in a few short and beautiful letters, four years before his death, made me understand (maybe dream?) that I too was a bearer of the sign.

Jean Fanchette
February 28, 1992

OSMOSES

(1954)

WORDS FOR TOMORROW

to Vincent Monteiro

I spoke to the stone
coiled in its thousand-year night
the language of light
I spoke to the birds
the shifting language of waters

I told the tall rooted trees
the slow adventure of fleeting clouds
and the rattled flight of pigeons
I told the seashells
tales of ships lost in the swell
the ageless longing of the sea

I sang for a strange girl
the murky poetry of bodies
the eternal return of times deceased
I told a child the legends of the night
and with him I'd have liked to believe
that dawn always starts anew…

and now the first star
is no more than the last lamppost.

FLED IS THAT MUSIC*

to Jean Courtioux

My soul is this November sky
With the trees' clasped liana-hands
Raised in what mystic leap?
My soul is an autumn softness
Sprung from your love's side
From my childhood retrieved
Asleep in rumor
Far from the absent sea

My soul is an immense dawn
That night has tempted in vain
That with a smile cracks open
My nostalgic autumn softness

But what bird has taken wing
Over on the hills of time
What harried flight of doves
In an inkling of fog?

---

* The title of this poem is in English in Fanchette's text.

Presto Vivace

to Raymond Lafaye

I'm always on the run I've never stopped
All done while running love and birth and death
I chase down suns I've never even seen
I run after dreams I'll no longer have

I catch the seasons in their endless cycle
of dazzling green, of metamorphoses
Time's not for me I keep watch on the clouds
Drifting behind them toward vague silences

A nameless meteor in the sky of ages
No longer even knowing the place I fled
in outer space I lead a hellish whirl
Of jeering phantoms who have never died.

September's Land

A cello moaning in September's hearth
So many sobs we've transformed into laughter
In vain time pounds this zone of memory
When the world's autumn brightens up your face

Autumn divided between gold and fire
September's oar shoves farther off the island
Over there the sea in motionless time
Scatters the fire of memory's sun

Forgetting, absence: they've cut up the heart
This land September's land
My firm steps on your secret path
Grasp your history.

THE POEM OF THE CHILD TREE

to Yvonne and
Robert Ganzo

The rhythmic pulses of a landscape
Vibrating in the veins of the tree,
The brother rock and his omens
Were grasped in the morning
Brought to me from the depth of ages.

The same bird from shore to shore,
Keeps the rhythm of lightning season.
The same rowboat cast adrift
Dreams of giddy desert heights
Of silences of water and stone.

The storm bursts and the child tree,
Coiled up in the wind's palm,
Understands our brotherhood
Sealed in the blood of summers.
Was I a larch? afterwards? before?

In the forests of memory,
Mankind plants his territories
And the child tree, born of storms,
Discovers the soul of leaves
Nestling in the evenings' heavy heart.

The tree remembers the seed,
The slow night of roots,
The forests of resin and shade,
Until the call of the first bird
Across centuries of waiting.

And I, the child of one second,
Amid the flowing gold of the broom bushes,
I watch over that moment set down
By the anguish of millions of years
In the world's bright disorder.

All these birds in my memory
And all these mallows in my eyes.
To transmute into moire and fire
The landscapes that were never
Better defined than far from here.

The tree that I call larch,
Changes into jacarandas,
Flamboyant, abloom in purple
Bursting in my blood, which weighs
The weight of all these seasons.

The oriole in the cherry tree,
The hummingbird in the mango tree,
And I, torn apart by your cries,
And I, suddenly discovering the price
Of living and fulfilling two lives.

Mountains of what memory?
I pick the grapes of your foresight.
At last I reach the clarity
Of minerals. Brief light
Where I discover this hand,
Held between the tree and the stone.

And the sand is once again seaweed
The manifold soul of the coral
Throbs, caught in the mesh
Of the water. The coal remembers
The forests and the childhood of fire...
All of it in a second's flash!

THE NOONS OF BLOOD

(1955)

The Noons of Blood

An autumn flower
for the grave
of Robert Edward Hart

Noons dissheveled
      in my memory's vault
Your shadows entangled
      on the Azur an assault

The gypsy with ripe wheat
      from autumn exiled
He sobs among the leaves
      with red blood sealed

Then father-killers gunned down savannahs
Suns and cicadas know a silent divide
Indian sea through becomings channeled

Tell me now to what nearby suicide
Runs the howling pack of unknown memories
And childhood to which dark stream of miseries?

The Adventure of Memory

to Édouard Besson

I never wanted to seek you elsewhere
Than in the nighttime crenels, Anguish, oh memory
With you I lived the childhood of the fountains
For you I unknotted the first day's dawn

I caressed the earth with ashen hands
When the forests' soul was not yet born
I lived the stone's exalting destiny
And captured with a glance the spring of fossils

Hence finally I invent that ancestral Woman
Who throbs without limit in millennial depths
Since I retrieved the hope of resurgences
In centuries bearing the reason of one day

As long as some willow tree
Lights up my memory
My steps of themselves will go
To battle against the hazards
And at that time I'll say
To the night of the outskirts
What remains of daylight

In the hands of childhood
What remains of starlight
In exile in the morning
And I will say the snow

The snow of distant ages
That quakes in the world's heart…

The night's children die in my memory
The black suns' soul is tenuous again.

What lasso of light has, implacable, caught
The green cathedrals in the wind's thick hair
The wandering billows with their ashy crest—

The forest of the birds blossomed unbound
Over midnights' blood at break of day.

AUTUMN

to Svetlana

I killed among the gold flecks in the autumn wind
summer's blond girl at my side
the blond girl who resembled memory
And the orioles in the alfalfa
sing the giddiness of warm evenings
Like your hoarse voice in the past my love
your voice of autumn crocuses and dead leaves
that still tastes of grapes stolen
from a heavy-hearted childhood…

Day-to-Day Dreams

to the dead Princess...

The other night, you were transmuted into a marble statue fixed to my table in a fleeting goodbye...That night the marble turned into translucent, iridescent ghost-flesh in the snow...

I walked with you on a distant shore that was lost in horizontal vertigo. A tiny grain of sand that was maybe a pearl made for the occasion was enough to make you stumble and slip into my immaterial arms.

I kissed you in the blue and almost palpable wind, under a wide sky tormented by autumn twilight, full of gulls and beating wings. I touched my lips to your lips. They had the weedy taste of spray across the water and the acrid flavor of unripe fruit...

The waters' breathing had quieted, drowned by your sighs. Immense waves of tenderness rolled over my body like useless sobs bringing a vaguely tinted hope into their backwash cloaked in foamy tatters...

Dawn revealed you walking aimless in the wet sand, far, far ahead of me, draped in your mysterious silence.

From deep in the Abyss, I flung my hands like tentacles toward the day...

Sprays of light bursting from the night.

Painful happiness of awakenings.

Crenels of dawn, as I woke up I saw steps in the snow. Nothing conveys loneliness more desperately than steps in the snow. Slowly I became aware of your absence...

and plunged headlong into the waking dream, into the grotesque and everyday whirl of living ghosts...

(January 29, 1954)

Song of Slow Longing

to Loys Masson

The Voice in the Desert said:

From corridor to corridor we walk implacably toward the light dragging along an ageless nostalgia as manifold as the sea. Strangers are our travel companions on morning sands moistened in pools of sunshine distraught at noon

The one who walked all day with me on the plain and called me his brother leaves me long before the Promised Mountain the mountain overlooks another plain as vast as my despair.

Millennia rustle in my veins

I remember a long night…
And Life is a seashell that Death makes sing

Sometimes a Snake torments me, one who has eyed me from prenatal depths And at noon I'm stuck with a baseless fear

Russet goodbyes of autumn twilights
What gypsy weeps in my brown blood
With my blind man's cane I feel around the slow night of the Abyss

Searching for a child dressed in light
Childhood mute yelp oh dream left behind

At night I have an appointment with Light in a no man's land fraught with impossible possible
And I speak to my ghosts. And I speak to my ghost
The language of silence
Like before

Then Light scatters and becomes fog
And I become fog
And everything starts anew

In the depth of long nights
I hear the baying of the Past
My soul remembers
A great mauve dawn

Thus spoke the Voice in the Desert. It had strangely monotone resonances and reached me in bundled murmurs like rustlings of sea-conches
I fell asleep harrowed with questioning. For all the Voice said was Questioning…

(December 2, 1953)

THE SONG OF APRIL

Since the same life will ever be intense
With the same words and with the same silence
Since your face was none other than the face
That loomed enormous in my ageless gaze
Since every face turned out to be your face
Since every season was only a long sigh
And the same wound ripped open at daybreak
Since blood was scared of water's innocence
Since water broke down into tears of sunshine
Since the soul feared awakening's abyss
Since night will never allow dawn to see
The secrets of delight in midnight's wells
Since night provides rest to its royal sadness
On the star-shaped fabric of spider webs
Since the hand held out between tree and sky
Will repeat the reason for torn-off blossoms
The scattered miracles of scarlet noons
Since every miracle is just the course
That links your eyes to the land's golden source

Since springtime passes through the sleeping city
Since April comes with its slow mystery
Since you instill in me a dizzy hunger
For the violent pureness of the earth
And since you have brought back onto my lips
A tang of ripe fruit and of dreams come true
And since you have put back into my pupils

Green tints of the possible Impossible
And since you have recaptured from the past
The sharp whiffs of a freshly cut wheat field
And a child whose features my memory immures…

Again I say your NAME in a virgin alphabet
Amazed as if this were the world's first morning
And I reinvent the Joy of long-gone ages
And with your gaze I relive Yesterday.

FOR A SPRINGTIME

to Philippe Chabaneix

I dream of springtimes on long-dead planets
Of mummified beauty on lost worlds
Of women aglow on the world's first morning
Whose sorry kisses linger on my mouth
Whose scent of wind and leaves hangs on my body
I dream of other women imprisoned in Time
Who wait to be born in mauve-tinted depths
Of Permanence enclosed in shadowy rings
Cradled in the bliss of coming springtimes
Present Past Future mysterious networks
Whose distant echoes stretch out into dreams
The Present a still-birth that my hands can't grasp
The Future a Woman coiled in rings of forgetting
Today in Yesterday Tomorrow in Today
I feel in my veins rustles of this moment's sap
And I drink the breath of dampened dawns
Which reaches me from what fossile springtimes
I dream of springtimes on long-dead planets...

I dream of heavy deserts of rustling wings
Where the numb sap congealed in mystery
Will still remember seasons that have passed
Symphonies of joy in air strewn with
Ancient miracles the stone makes eternal
And I see in my sky the green surprise
Of the world's earliest dawn
Soaring above the blue hills of time
Like a flashing spray of light.

Cycles and more cycles Life and Death forever
I see you again this evening my eyes wide open
Between Yesterday and Tomorrow endless trajectories
And I a witness with no mark of age
In my clarity brew the mystery of living

And trembling I grasp millennial springtimes
Scattered in the silence to which all things return.

MANHOOD

to the memory of my mother

Silence is blind to the fire of solitudes
and night is mute to the shipwreck lookout
Childhood is gone, impossible to relive
and God has withdrawn to heaven's highest reaches
Time fades into the grave memory of men...
Never more will the forest of birds peck away at dawn's thick
    flesh...
Never more will the aging Magi bring me their nostalgic gifts
    in the inn of the stars,
Never more...
Only the violins of Exile
and my mother's faraway voice behind the hills of absence.

To relight the flame in midnight's wells
it's no longer enough for me to touch my lips to the sun's wound
in the astounded flesh of my love.

In my rumorless heart
the autumns doze
and alone I head out for the same departures
dragging through the dust of my young dreams
my ageless, countryless, seasonless steps.
And thus to silence,
to the end of the night
with my memory full of suns...

(Mauritius, August 1954)

Archipelagos

(1958)

The Foam Liturgy

I

I sold my season to the coffee merchants.
So you didn't grow old sooner, my summertimes!
In the morning street, a well makes gurgling sounds
Fragile and threatened as long as daylight shimmers.

I traveled the world on the runway of gazes,
An archangel imprisoned in a suburban paradise
Where all the wandering trains came together,
Willing exiles from the stations of goodbye.

Hand gestures, foam liturgy,
In my head millions of summers collide
And each has paid its price in water and wind.
A leaf has taken the sacrament of daybreak.
Daybreak has rowed along memory's shore
And all my archipelagos have burst their moorings.

II

So that the water's litanies return to sandy mysteries,
Savannah of silence motionless in high wind,
Where the bird whirls and screeches in its own shadow,
Trellises of ripe time, oh seasons alive with water,

And so that the eye gets hitched to daybreak's fork,
To forgotten heights, to daylight's ocher drift,
Deep time digs in like seeds of a new earth
And summer's female rancor quiets down.

III

On the Congo River, the hyacinths drift.
Africa hurts me as it names my exile.
I'm the one left on the shoreline's fringe
Dazzled by departure, stupefied by sunshine.
On the ground of Imerne, red birds die.
I keep watch, alongside the foam cathedrals.

Africa hurts me. Taking over my seasons
Its fog of light imprisms my memory
And edges toward the deep daylight of the marsh
Calm in wind and water, my sleeping roots.
What's left of daybreak on the bloody lookouts
Is shrouded silence with its shivers of algae.

Scorned Africa, hoarse Africa, Africa,
My share of Negritude hitched to the summers
Tows a nameless regret. I'm not from here
And only the tree knew how to find my secrets.
A rush of water swells on memory's day:
On the Congo River, the hyacinths drift.

IV

The naked woman's body quartered at daybreak,
Where the river forks on its way to the estuary,
Calms the docile storm, assigns to daylight
The crippled hour pregnant with slumber.
A blink of eyelash and all the worlds move:
Black blood's midnights dream of further exile.

To leave here nameless where all is slow escape!
I bump against bars forged from recollection.
The other memory keeps implacable watch.
Skies learned in vain, and with a tragic movement
They drain the constellations' alphabet.
Harnessed to exile I spell a wide mauve sky.

But nothing has soiled the harsh, the bitter love
And one by one the mourning cities shelve
Their fast-paced lying and sonorous feasts.
Memory has a shadowy gap at best
Overlooked by masks that no one lifts.
On the Congo River, the hyacinths drift.

V

Cathedral with wind filling its happy sails,
Right where the spire of dawn set the time,
The daylight fully rises decked in omens.
Foam prayers afloat on epic gasps
What road traveled to the ports of tenderness,
Amid what rumors of hot night and insects?

The unique and boundless landscape reaches up
To the transhumant azure of memory's depths.
The secret navigation of a childhood
Reappears in the broad glow of life embraced
As a perspective of escapes and returns
Under a changeless sky of traveling peaks.

In its substance, then, in vain the final cry
Takes form and fights against the vice of daylight.
A childhood of exile dead without burial
Sets forth. And still the wide suspended sky
The russet roofs and wind caught in the masts,
The hill stretched out and panting, pink at dawn.
Must the child die and childhood live?

On the Congo River, the hyacinths drift.

MEMORIAL

to Claude Fanchette

Fragile, the memory in men's hearts
Courses its way to the high resurgence
Of water and sap where the daylight starts
Like a season left behind in autum's radiance.
In the heat of memory the heart is spent,
Space breaks free and chars the moment.

The clarity of the forgotten desert,
My hands clasp the bundled sheaves
Of sage and autumn's sad wheat leaves.
The night has left its parables scattered
In confused gestures, in brief preamble
Where hand, water, and pitcher all tremble.

Sitting happy under the woundless sky,
Amid murmurs a memorial dies.
I walk alone in shadowy forests
In the possibility of childhood's vale,
Among the transparencies I sail
And I dance the river in its summer's secret.

My first season was inhabited
By the well-wrought silence of the sea.
For a long time my cathedrals drifted
In the burned-out traces of a summer.
So that in his glimmers my eyes shed their leaves
I watch out for that child trapped in murmurs

And under midnight's fleeting glow,
In the rocky springs of sifted stars.
Then a face sets sail and with its stares
Unlocks the sky's forbidden sites
And orchards that taste of green mango.
On my lips childhood again alights.

On the steady runway of shipwrecks,
I waited, minding the landscapes,
For the first ship's arrival. It came rigged
With all winds and with all hopes
Under the mauve sky of my heart's anchor
And I chose exile in back of the mirror.

Pilgrimmage in the woods of September.
A bird gets caught in the net of its migrant
Name. A tree, turning red, intrudes on me and
Lives all alone in the glow of amber.
The sectors of my life have found their reasons
And fall draws golden light from other seasons.

ARCHIPELAGOS

to Mark Ward

I

The path runs over to the sabbath of
The birds. And through the invulnerable night, off
To the side of the foam fields the Vedic secret sits.
Trapped in the drifting archipelagos, it musicates
The hunger of an eternal that can't be fed.
Amid the water's gestures, birth, life, and death
Intertwine here and on the blank pages
Of this scattered night, a lone rower emerges,
Crowned with kelp and blinded by glimmers.
To the storm of the world his silence simmers
With the liturgy of the ocean's whisper.
A cerulean braid of dawn has tied
The forest's rumors to the calming tide
And palms are already dancing in the luster.

II

Far off, oh nebulous one exiled in her name,
From an ever-shifting capital we came,
We who refuse to live in the legends,
Rites, and secrets of the sea and sands.
Lost as I am to childhood's bitter cause,
I send back to the orchards icy with loss
The transylvan homage of plucked strings,
Long ripened by a hot summer in suspense.
The watchful voyage from earliest daylight
To the sky's full ribbing at slumber's height
Carries me. Here I am, mingling with the roots,
Where the moment in profile keeps the sealed moment out:
A tear glistens on the eyelashes of the passing wind
And through lattices of space the gulf lets light in.

III

Briefly surging up through the radiance
Of a memory shimmering like moon diamonds
The last forest is still on fire below ground
And the traces of embers blind the moraines
Where the icy wind bites into the birds' hearts.
I walk in comfort on the waters' slumber.
In solidarity I agree, hardly surprised,
To travel back toward this dockside
Of dreams and leaps either named or mastered
And time reconnects with forgotten gestures:
Suddenly I grasp what indefinable plan
Brought the young ocean to tame the sand
And what remorse arises from the heart of the isles
When the migrating bird heads back into exile.

IV

If bubbles of tender day swarm into sunbirds
From dim algae in the wild maze of slumber,
What precious silence gathers in its tow
Briefly burning from underground forests' glow?
The river rises and remakes itself from the azure
Consumed by crystals where space measures
The span of the gesture bursting its bounds.
And the first truth glistens all at once.
Our eyes will burn in the golden brilliance
Of a dream docking on its own resilience:
Daylight is no longer daylight and time's pulses
Will shrink away in the ponds, useless.
Of an old dream we're the last survivors,
Remembered only by our footsteps on the shores.

EXILES

for Ervin Neuhaus

The traveling pollens and the birds in transit,
Everything drives me to the exile not in exile.
The same landscape lights along my eyelids
The Sporades, Upper Egypt with a tiger smile,
The evening's cobalt blues on slender schists.

When the night dropped its rumors on the corals
Idioms sang their way through the palm trees
And the wind offered up its brief parables
To the blue sharks asleep in the calm streams.
What snow trail has abandoned the symbols?

When the night unloaded its long caravans
Beersheba blazed deep within the mauve sands
And the harp gave out as it played a pavana.
All the fires of exile lit up the savannah
And the corpse-filled night took the sky's beige hands.

Since then, I await, in the evening, the parting islands.

Provisional Identity

(1965)

The Four Elements

for Lawrence Durrell

I

Durable. The one who foams on this shore's neck,
Pulse on fire, carries the species along.
The sun burning in the fetishes' heart
Will trace through the sky the mirage's start.
The first one up sings the matins song
While dancing above the shipwrecks;
The winds, all the winds on the horizon graze
Like herds of deer that go fleeing away.

Flowers pop out of the mouths of the dead
And the sea fills up with ancient absence.
The poles send the dawn right into harm
And the moment dies in its incandescence.
Fueling the fleeces, what fiery arm
Of a dark world wakes up the blood?
The day sets sail far from eyes and ears,
My voice's echo will wait a thousand years.

II

At times the wind, in big green murmurs
Lights up and dons punctured tints.
Even the desert sands, needing no rain,
Go thirsting after knotted veins.
Coming late to the forests in rumors
Murky reason takes joy's breath away.
We won't get far if the wind relents;
Under the drooping tree, fruit will decay.

May September once more walk in vines
And a figure with its number be aligned,
The unlearned words from exile return
Like the Magi full of interest and insight.
Suns with arrowhead beams will burn
The eyelashes of those who refuse light.
One day a boat arrives on the shore
And the organ musicates in the stone's core.

III

The ocean yaps where the broom was in flower
And the boat stem shouts with laughter and tears.
From an ancient landscape blurred by a shower,
The echo soars and clasps the silent years.
On the plains of water, its sweet face afloat,
The evening sketches my love in soot.
The seagull needs the storm in order to sleep:
My love has discovered its landscape.

Our armadas capsize in seizures.
A single anchored ship justifies
The sun, the ancestral burst of laughter;
The sky still staggers and mystifies
Foam faces with their lifeless stare.
The vacant lots on the sea reject
Every hope and every regret:
I shipwrecked my heart on sad pleasures.

IV

No longer death, the zone of slumber
That a steep dream delivers in number,
A trail of shadows at the sun's hollow,
A driving flame the eye doesn't quite follow.
The earth's wind plainsings to the swell:
The origin is the reef that two seas pound.
All the diamonds of memory resound
And a crystal plays arpeggios on the shells.

The day has lived dangerously.
From my pen an element takes form,
But I no longer know if it's on the anvil
Of language that the flame of blood swirls
Or at the heart of the orchards of foam.
The expanse of a word impels the world's
Parentheses to explode and it kindles
What we still give the name of clarity.

(1957)

HABIT OF EXILE

for my father

I

But no more nerves remaining on the face
To take account of the wind's steady pace
On the fork of time run all aground
The blind bird has completed its round

Our dead are quicker than the quick
Left naked under the squall of the isles
The snow is dirty on the plains of exile
In the vacant lot a grassy leprosy
Blasphemes to a springtime whispered as sick
The very farthest from the happy memory.

II

The frescos of fog in the gray cities
Fade in the night that is no longer time
A mysterious identity realigned
In the sketches of transhumant sleep
And a breeze offered in the name of high seas
And syllables of an age once kind
I see the children of light as they leap

On their braids the ocean pounds and creeps.

III

Sap stuck in the tree's enduring pains
Not suspended on the marble staircase
A minute outside of time will assume
The day's perfect destiny in the foam
And the water's music seals with space
All the sea that a shell contains

Time upright in its own bright flashes
Taught us that no other exile exists.
Tomorrow we'll need to unlearn summer's gist
And refuse the world beneath our eyelashes.

IV

Through cracks the old sea song calling
Who taught us exile? And these pollens
A lofty passenger in the musical trees
To get burned on the hard salt of the reefs?
May this time die as I cast it out
May my memory's crystal fade out
My eyes shut to the pages that I read
The slow stride of writing on a mirror
Suspending the night draws exile nearer

OF ANOTHER COUNTRY

The herd of the winds overtakes sleep
The devasted country and this abrupt love
Your body the rowboat turns toward its nighttime port
And the fire down there that burns out

This readable face that resembles
So many other faces I'd like to deny it
But on the edge of your hand run aground
I dream of the war's springtimes

Outside the massacre begins
I'm among those who will fall

SEASONS

to Zvi Milshtein

What Africa in clamors pains my belly
When soft-green April scatters its rumors,
And what russet storm in tears in the forests?
Here, the watchful eye receives the fallow sky:
I no longer know what to call the gesture's span
The dodge and the leap of the primal tree.

In the almond the roots already strain,
It's the earth reaching farthest for survival
But the sun gets trapped in its own lies...

Too many birds in the sky from out of the Gospel,
Too many arms in the orchards refuse revolt.
Where I live the earth moves halfway to the sky
And the wind gets ripped apart in the crook of the trees.

I hate your springtime decked in fragile lace.
At the virile time pushing through the bark,
I'll come back to bruise your wine harvests,
When the grass is greener on the tombs,
When in the haggard daylight of your landscape
The summer will be as hoarse as anger's jab.

(1957)

Refusal of the Death Instinct

to Elisabeth Janvier

A mouth whose smile opens to the redder blood of wounds
And gypsum hands with no reflections I already sense your
    death
Moving deep inside me in the smoke of the tall grasses

And since I tie you, fragile and irreplaceable, to death
A presence sitting at the edge of my age I know the port
From the dull sobs of dawn, I'm with you all through the day
An eternal lifetime in the clearest brightness of my body.

But now time throws its sands and handfuls of shadow in our
    eyes
For night to be our vassal, serving humble very humble,
For winter not to be remorse, inhabited by penitent trees.

In November, the mustangs invaded the City
And their hoofs sparkled the incendiary leaves.

It was in a former life
And death prowled, transparent, in November
To tear the tart love from its seed.

He stretches out across the dark earth
And it's not dying

He resumes dialogue with the dark earth
And the night of habitual roots

And now the rivers flow into his blood
The estuary once again promised.

It's the measure of gray time,
The wind risen over there far away
Like here in the place with no memory
A gesture: the grave certainty of playing
The whole life all at once,
Here in the place with no face
Where fear quietly fades out
Among the paths that came up from the sea.

I refuse to give the day my strongest faithfulness.
I take on the freedom of the sand on the sea.
I stay awake. There's no other voice to defeat me.

He's there in the dark room
Light coming up from his fingers.
He doesn't know what sleeping is
He's the one who bears sleep.
The gray of years has emptied his gaze,
The waves of rumors break on his shore.
He no longer knows what dying is
Open to the wind that comes from elsewhere,
That senses the earth and the calm waters.

Tomorrow dizziness inhabits his face.

ITINERARIES

I

to Suzanne Campbell-Jones

The waste lands past, it's the dawn
Marked by the etching of sage.

Every week and not every day
I surface to woe.
Its waves wear out on the curve of Sundays.

Smells of yet another new city,
Death in the incisures of the plane trees.
I dig through other summers with no echo:
Faces borrow from faces.

But the music has remained faithful to its dizziness:
A lame movie organ, a saxophone's hoarseness.
London. The city is an immense roastery
Whose walls alone stay standing.

II

to Pierre Clerc

Emtpy lots came from the long absence
In which nothing grew but nettles and iron.
And it was December. And the night fermented
In its holds.
And the soul staggered.

Blood in its certain flow told time.

But when night changed regimes
No eyelash-batting in the sky
Announced the daybreak to the lookouts
And the tall grass kept quiet.

Death came calling.

He inhabits the night. He's inhabited by the night.
And his blind hand crushes the purest form
Elsewhere, the pink of the sands flashes in the light.

III

for Valérie

The smell of the wind in a high chamber
The smell of the dry straw in summer
The illuminated ship sliding toward the estuary
All that finally keeps death away,
All will be offered to you.

The night will be mild in the sheepfolds
At the hour of your choosing,
The towpath gets lost in the woods.
Your steps by themselves will find their shore
In the regions of nondying.

Rather the fraternal grayishness reserved by the beech trees
In the lands that you loved,
Than the light flowing to the secrets of the stained-glass
    window,
To take arms against tomorrow.

Rather, even, the rainy landscapes of doubt.

IV

to Anita Bachmann

What does all death aim for, shores
Discovered among the dawn's bulrushes,
When will we land on the high dynasty of the cliffs?

Day after day our realm runs dry
And every liturgy is recognized as a fable.
Even silence is captured weapons in hand.

The distance from earth to night is too short
And the day between sleep's eyelashes too brief.
To resist,
Just once have we sacrificed
To the uncontradictable lie
As sharp as summer's sword.

Since then we survive, we survive.

V

For the night,
The rumors you track down, the rumors in your footsteps,
Have no importance.

The night tames you.
It surrounds your most dangerous silences.

You'll get dizzy from lights,
Then at three in the morning,
You'll feel your heart abruptly age.
Your squandered castle will abruptly fade into the dark water.

So it is that no step
Will any longer match yours.
You'll have to walk, walk some more,
Your eyes burdened with grasses.

STATIONS

to the memory of Guy Bréda

I

Two bright oars barely move sleep
On the slope where I stop.

Slowly,
                    The landscape that fell apart
Comes back together.

Pure vestiges, the morning unchangeable
On the taciturn disorder of the saxifrages.

II

Clearings in the distance among the trees
And morning struck by the geometries of frost.

Here on the path where every voice breaks
What fire in the first surprise of awakening!
Who knew that this fire would burn
As far as the hard mineral of wanting?

We send signals, we shout.
No one's there to see us,
No one hears us.

III

Dizziness and will of the perfectible morning
Summarize the combat we've waged.
The smoke falls apart on the stormy ground,
There's no more reason to betray the silence.

So very much was needed, in this glacial land
Where a soul on fire gets caught in frost,
Where shadow blocks light more quickly
In back of the gaze. So many seasons were needed
For us to be sure of our territories,
This bit of ground, a field of rye and alfalfa
For the unstored summer.

To last. All weapons turned outward,
To the heart the greatest distance.

And break the clumsy flight of the bird migrating toward death.

IV

Don't let yourself get caught in the sweetness of the stops
In the evening in the ports
When in the distance the high-sea
Ship of death passes.

Winter. A dead deer eyes wide open
At the edge of an icy pond,
There's your landscape
And its sparks cold in the iron trees.

REALM

to John Forrester

Language surrounds the empty cities of dawn
The frugal light, the abraded countryside
(Prunings in the thickness of broad daylight)
And the sign redeems the lost origin.

A calm decree of the basalts,
Glyphs of the absent word.

to Jean Bessil

These lines
Which define no form
Situate the origin and its obscure power

The hard mineral fish
Swims in the nighttime marlpit

Real possible alienation
Are no more than words taking distance

Flint lifts the sparks
Of a name without a country

Every word before me reties itself
To the tree on which my bark is summarized.

YESTERDAY TRANSPARENCY

Palm against palm
But between them inaccessible transparency

There's the sea surely there's the sea
But the returning ships got stuck in the sand
And the broom bushes beat the boat stem
Absence is on the prow

Beyond this moon-sun the night that I seek
And that isn't night
Farther than this voice that trembles and breaks

My itinerary doesn't necessarily pass through these summits
    that you invent every day
I walk quite simply

There was the time
When every blade of grass protected me
I reconstructed the faces in the clay of days
The gray foam of hands beat in vain on the windows
I was
I moved ahead on the banks and in the evening I knew that my
    drifts would carry me to the estuary of broad daylight

Today I no longer know the rivers' direction
Far from the sea I attend to day-to-day business

The grass

The star-twinkling of just one flower across the light-years

The wind that rises and puts down the wheat of the coming harvest

The landscape readable yesterday with a blind person's fingers.

On what forgotten field did I store so many treasures

Say my four-year-old child on the bank of the same river

(June 1965)

to the memory of Nadia Vebov

You'll come, time undoing the crowing of the red roosters,
You'll come.
In the old shadow together we'll spell
The hard syllables of dying.

The sound of our footsteps will softly fade
And the wheel of the seasons on the barren heath;
Far beneath the sky a large flock of white birds
Will again plunge on habitual misfortune

As in this antique life.

Ambivalence of the Place

to Annie and Francis Lohéac

I

The grass And even fire has gestures of grass
On the habitual road my room without echoes
Caught in the highest brightness of our gestures

A little blood soaks this face

The last tree has left the last bird
The sky casts off far away from the last cloud
This dawn the fire is white on the back of the dimmed countries
Where the tides will no longer come yapping

Darkly the fire raises the daylight
Darkly the fever pounds our shore

II

Landmark

The falcon sun on morning's fist
Finally casts off on the orchards of light
Water is the first to unlearn baptism

It's raining softly on the cities of salt
The large faces sculpted in the wind
Go down toward the sea

III

Carousel of shadows it's you again
Tormenting this back country of memory
In the June night darkly run aground

Silence pounds this arid place of mankind
The last constellations fly low over the sea
Already absence surrounds absence

The dragnet in the dark water gathers its nighttime nuggets
O flow and ebb of hope.
And there you are silent your head filled with clamors

IV

Landmark

Hammered (and infinitely gushing)
On this promontory where the night shatters

Murmurred (and infinitely invented)
Here's the homeland of forgetting
Defined by the just word

The patient writing of the shadow on the stelae

V

The red-breasted merganser turns in the devastated sky
(Captive of a root people and false signals
O moment's torn one)
Nighttime fear weighs on the lowlands

Here the moment writes the desert landscape I invent
Standing in the fire of the torrent you live
You no longer know of the night lying at the base of the day

And the water of this face that time was drinking

VI

Over the silent land the wind my allegiance
Chases out the spark shavings
That yesterday were caught in winter's forges

I'm rowing in the ocean of ryes

The childhood dwelling flees beneath the horizon
The wind a race captain
Relegated to the inland grounds
Works the dunes in a dream
The wind finally rips out the day at the bottom of the day

This copper sky sprung from what memory
Down in childhood's Finisterre
It's always six p.m.
In that coastal town
Caught in the fires of the last sun

I hear the packs withdrawing toward the sea

Over the silent lands the wind my allegiance
Awakens the dawn the fallow the real
The house from here navigates in the murky brightness
The rumors of childhood shatter and die

I lost Every defeated one is promised to the fire
I burn with you naked woman torch inverse
In the ever nocturnal river of the bed

The Towpath

I

Going to the end of the towpath
Even if it leads into shadow
The scattered body will know how to provide its own light
Extreme sparks in the extreme chamber of the possible

II

Shepherdess of sleep
Companion of my wandering toward the vivid peaks
I've long been a refugee in this enclosure of disaffected time
Long a prisoner of the parceled land
Today I escape
Forcing the harrows of the rain falling on Flanders
Come desert with me

Silent she comes crossing the echoless night
She's already on the dark plaza when death catches up with her

III

The aerie expands with the bird spinning in the kingdom of its
    own fright
The last sunflower's eye fades out
Time will come apart under the night of the eyelids

For a long time we'll walk in the last ardor of the sands

We won't go far out on the promontory
Where tirelessly the wind erases
The writing of the broom bushes
The sky's roadbed at eye level
The space burning among the sails
From afar we'll wave

And then don't ask the name of this land
Granted to our footsteps that have no more memory

IV

It's the last morning caught in the riverbanks' reflections
A long patience has broken our moorings
So many lost ships are well worth a voyage
Though we'd sworn to go back up the rivers

The reconquered space will have to be populated
With naked hands and with gestures from this former life
So that so much absence isn't so much absence

A face decipherable under the silk of kisses
Listen come from afar the wind that ruins
Time and branches Listen to the clamors
Of the wind that no longer knows how to dispossess the heart

V

In turn the wind fills up this mouth
Of the sandy shadows
Its gaze goes into exile and no longer knows how to read
Our shared landscapes

Dawn giddily sets up the desert
Flint and stormy ground and we traps of fire

VI

Pure and dryly vibrating flash
In the sleeping sky where time drops its flowers
It's the same sun it's the same titmouse
It's our death's fiery tongue

The light has dissolved our empty lands
The avalanche of memory booms nearby

VII

For a long time we've walked

        toward this antique province

May the rock be rock

        like it has no face

In vain have we deciphered

        this very old grief

May the wind be wind

        like it has no memory

(January 1965)

AGAMEMNON'S TOMB

to the memory of Gustave Regler

Neither the end of the night nor the vertical recovered
Under the downpour of the days
Could conquer dizziness
Nor this motion of islands capsizing in the dawn

The faded word your season in mysterious reprieve
While the high flowers of death were unfolding
It was necessary to refuse the dark angel and his inverse
    landscapes
To struggle against the dark city where November had planted
    its crosses
While in the devastated zone of your exile all escape was
    becoming laughable
Then the reality of Mycenae was given to you

Outmoded ocean   then white sun
        on the road to Mycenae
When the triremes of music rounded the promontory
In order
        to tame equalizing death and its dark silence
Eternally caught in the trap of our four arms
Go stranger on the road to Mycenae
And don't refuse to hear Agamemnon's voice
When winter's decree sharpens the distressed fallows
And light raises light
(Pure vestiges music of time on the harp of the hills
Rocks plunging toward the first secret
Trees once again mixing with the rock)

The waves of light infinitely garnish it

(Cry of the protruding rock that refuses its gangue
Trill fading in the bird's throat
O flower eternally folded by the light)

The moment finds its bearings in calmed time
First sounds of the day among the ryes
O death of death
In order to eternally pound the bright gold of our shores

Each lost sign is a forgotten world
Where the fire of mankind gushed into the rock
The rock will never again be faceless

In order
  to eternally question equalizing death
Go stranger on the road to Mycenae
Among the wild ryes and the shattered rocks
The time that's no longer time will take you by the hand
The taciturn olive tree will tell your adventure
Which is the exile of the world

The coiled day travels in the ellipse of the day
The nighttime sea pounds against the faded word
Against the promontories of the word
These bleached vestiges of time bleached vestiges of wind
Line up in the place of memory
Align against nighttime death

O Greece outline traced on the relieved sky
Pure gesture stopped among the graves

Greece you were saying was the name of our absence
The nettle hasn't grown into this absence
And the traveling sky that denies all absence

As long stranger as the little music of your life comes apart
As your steps get heavier on the abraded ground
The ocean rumor fills up the vastness of this sky
Hardly weighing on the prone millennia more alive than the
    living
On the boulders where light's slender javelins break

And on this promontory bathed in youth
    Eternally
Once again you approach lost reality
You agree It's enough for all the clamors to fade out
And for death to be your vassal in eternal time

And now the triumphal ship of day is approaching
The tombs in the torn light have abolished death

(1965)

MY NAME IS SLEEP

(1977)

for Frédérique

"While asleep, all men collaborate as brothers
on the world's becoming."
Heraclitus

THE INVERTED EYE

to Michel de M'uzan

The inverted eye lighting
My blind landscape
Sweeping the forgetful walls
Of the tunnel-past
Through which I escaped.

The grass fire the combes
The grain of sand wet with saliva
At the far limit
Of the land of nonexile
The silver leaf pressed
In the book of travel
The desperate pilgrimage

Of the little soldier in the bitter foam
All the salvos on the shore of
The ocean of memory
In the early morning of childhood.

Now the night. The combes again
That this Southern night blurs
The bombardment on the coral bar
The grief soon covered up
By the alluvial singing...
A sail on this undefinable
where when how word
From what birth.
Opacity-living transparency-dreaming...

In order to finally decipher the unreadable word
The sign on the starry windowpane of sleep.

An awakening a break in the continuum
In the maze of hours
The beheaded cliff of the interrupted dream
Leans toward the difficult day.

Beyond the garden of frost
The low-lying house in which the fiery tongue
(the lamp) watches over the dead child.
In the mineral branches
The red sun
Watching over this world that in turn will die.

And the cymbals of dawn smothered
by decisive evidence.

PLURAL FACE

to Véronique D. F.

I

Beyond the end of the alphabet
The only recourse: maybe the capital letters of the bird in the
    wind
But the inverted sky had blurred
the furrows of the clouds
The trees were made of iron and winter burned there
I had reached the confines of the empty land.

O plural face
Beating just below the curtain of the rain
In the flickers of the laughable springtime.

Landmark I

The Foreign Woman has come into my dwelling
Corral of the animals of sleep
The turning flower of shadow
The rose of the winds from the land of memory

II

The bird finally veers from the squadron of misfortune
Relieved I walk under its fragility
The swell of the days breaks against your only word.

In the bruised thickets of February I find back
The difficult traces of stubborn footsteps
Heading toward this heath runway of the West Wind.

The bit of smoke contained in your hands
Will weigh heavier than the reserves
Ever renewed in time
Between the parentheses of the solstices.

Landmark II

On this dark heath
Where the word "heath" is a breath of some November
Crosses oh crosses time
Populates this space of the voyage back.

III

The castles of the Rue Chernoviz
Blaze in the fog
After is already started
In the unbreakable patience of the lavas
Down there.

Wo es war, soll ich werden

On her way is the one who was lost
Opening the coveted clearing
In the low and somber forest of the days.

IV

When the ship crested with wind capped with foam
Returns to port
Cleared is the bar of habitual misfortune
Left behind are the shallows of desire
Deaf to sirens
The heart

(When summer confronts the flint
to steal the sparks concealed in its desire)

When the hardening lavas reserve among their braids
faces for the eternity that is rock
And the time to die will only be this bird
torn to stillness under the sun of carnage

Then in the cave of shadow under the cliff's red awning
The rose will turn again.

Landmark III

The machine guns of the rain
In this kindly garden
Where yesterday the rose of May was turning...

There will be survivors:
The virile laurel, the medlar
And the woodpecker that questions the tree
The insect that flows in the woods
And the thirsty heart.

V

So this evening again comes pounding
This forgotten unlearned wave
Against my life in tears.
Faithful and unfaithful companion
of my season of anger
Love, listen to December's cello
in the dimmed hearth.
The fire that we were has lost its homeland
This name where I lived.

VI

Maybe you'll have to hold your breath
You in turn held under the mauve awning of dizziness
(Why do all these years seem garnished
with a mauve thread:
the color of death and of the wind in Mycenae
the color of this fruit burst under the sun of Africa
that you didn't want to touch?)

Maybe you won't need to fear crossing swords
against her word.
She's watching for your weakness ready to bite
Ready to destroy you.

But her body turns like a rowboat
Caught in the bed's rapids.
Death waves to both of us
In the clamors of our silence
O readable to my blind man's fingers.

Landmark IV

The blind finger on bare skin
Traces
The hieroglyphics that tame
Death.
The nighttime hand gathers and receives.
It doesn't know how to give.
Nothing should be given to death.
This gives it an appetite.

VII

It won't be any more difficult
Thus leaning on Tomorrow surprised
To seek in the muddy tidal bore of the days
This face that was undone.
Maybe the line of the obstinate jawbone
will be harder
The dizziness of the pleading gaze
More ashen.

The ironic smile will rise from the whirlpool
And drink me

Oval that dissipates the questioning
As does *devastation* Strindberg's doubts
Oval in the water dream's river
Oval in the nighttime river

From what memory
The water and this egg of the origin?
These beats of the music of the origin
Satellites of the end and the beginning
Before the perfect wearing away?

SADE AT LA COSTE

to Jean-Max Toubeau

The fossile scorpion dies again on the breach of summer
Sade (Sad for me)
Twice revived under the disorder of the rocks
No longer propped on the night of Vaucluse
He travels in the word
While his dwelling is now only a sketch
His presence the oblique shadow on a slab
That's gaining on the night.

PLACES

to Paul Rasse

I

October behind the gray foam of the window known as five o'clock in the evening. In the living room, under the still un-lit chandelier, the waves widen from the silence. The moment is like an orant. The street's calming down. A single gust has ruined autumn's branches. The leaves, heavy with their own death in the damp twilight of Avenue Mozart, pile up on the sidewalk that's swept by the bloody streaks of the lit-up signs…

II

On the road between Thiers and La Chaise-Dieu, the pines and larches rooted in the snow, swaying, surprised in the glow of the headlights, like twitching animals, awakened in the sheepfold too long before dawn…

III

In the light sleep of dawn, I discover the cities of the plain...A droning voice like that of the muezzin who woke me up in Dar es Salaam suddenly changes tone and shouts: "The Sasanians, the Sasanians are here!"

IV

Crève Cœur is unchangeable to him. The low-lying house, the orchard, the lopsided lawn are on borrowed time. Tomorrow, this old volcanic ground will reclaim its rights and, after the passing of mankind, will once again dialogue with the wind, the impassible sky that weighs on the Indian Ocean.

V

The storm rode the mare called Paris.
No one knew where it would be thrown.
The autumn rodeo celebrated the glorious
                    death throes of the forest.
(O whelks of death)
October went back up the river.

VI

From here (Crève Cœur in Mauritius) La Nicolière Lake is like a slate eye shaded by the eyelashes of dreams, this species of copper green water lily. Women make a fuss when they pick them, for dreams here are edible…

VII

Ulysses in your travels…	Happier
Foam	the shadow
The insistent tiredness	that travels
of the waves	tirelessly
And finally the sails	through the space
of the earth	of the sundial

VIII

Cornwall. Land of West Penwyth crushed by summer. We minuscule ones coming into summer. And already the black comma of death on the vibrant page of the day.

IX

But in Bruges, the bells spoke the death of the rocks and death in the bisecting wind.

X

Saint-Venant. It's a question of number. A thousand deaths: defeat. Victory: five thousand who escape.

The world isn't insane because the psychiatric hospitals are filled with absence, resignation, and the pain that has no more tears.

Millions of survivors cruise in the light beyond the bars.

Just one isn't enough to darken the sun.

THE NORTH SIDE AND THE SOUTH SIDE

to Jean Hélion

I

Forty years!
The triumphant rage of having lasted
And of having made the leaping foam last.
The field of islands harvested
The nighttime triangle harvested
The angel has tamed the mirror's distortions.

II

And the winter that doesn't want to die!
The ravens weigh on the vacant lot
I hear as if from a forge
The gasping of the imprisoned buds.
I wait at the edge.
The deaf labor of the body
Defeats all desire.
The morning milk among the birches
Exhausts the gaze.

I wait at the edge.

III

If he were only the reflection
of his own abolished
     return
If I were the mirror

The jasmine the lip
The rain the scarf of fog

What's left is the seated lava
     to surround
If I were the midnight

IV

I speak the language of the loosened rocks returned to the abyss
The speech of rock in windy death.

I listen to the waterfall sound of this other speech that cradles
     the traveler surprised by the uterine night.

Blind swimmer heading from the estuary to the source...

V

The grass in the wind from here testified for the voyager tree
about the voyage back to the childhood land.

The wounded rock hasn't resisted the stammered word
eternally renewed
Childhood
Neither the heavy gunfire of the sea on the crests
    of Souillac
nor the nighttime moan of the Terral
And the bulbul always calls
In the great lilacs of memory.

VI

Torn tearing
In the night appellant of signs
in the torn night of signs

And on the waste land
(yesterday)
I the dealer in empty words.

VII

This reddish glow down there on the black silk
of the Southern night
(the childhood rowboat that gently tips over
    farther
toward the same South)
What residual speech!
And who comes this way walking on the water
Beneath the green glow of the lighthouse?

VIII

Everything suddenly becomes clearer
As at the end of the show when the stage
    lights up
Everything suddenly becomes more urgent
But no one wants to leave

…They don't know the theater's on fire.

THE CLOVERS

Remember this surprised street that went up from the city
Amid the swell of the morning grasses
Up to this clawed aloe field at the foot of the mountain
Where they burned fatalist Hindus
In the smell of lard and green beefwood.

Remember the school open to the four winds
Amid the clovers...

Fear of the beloved-brother with bludgeon fists
Who taught you the whirlwind of numbers
The smell of the dried ink and unrolled maps.

Since then

You've deconsecrated the chapels

The equalizing wind is no longer accountable for the shreds of
childhood

Words are once again words in the worn web of rituals

And your lamp has burned out in hands that have become

Fists of anger.

Hallelujah!

AFFIDAVIT

to the memory of Marcel Cabon

The last fibers of my belonging
Are ripped away one by one by the kora player.
The last moan of my allegiance
Is detailed by the twangy voice of the griot.

I told you I'm not from here
The deaf movement of my muscles lets me know each day
And this reddish dizziness of what forgotten archipelagos
Where the rose of shadows turns.
Surely my blind footsteps would recognize
The sands of Riambel
My feet would tame the scorched earth
And the Indian Ocean could wash away
The dust of Europe
In a unique sacrament of dawn.

But your wars are no longer mine
Your fighting words make me laugh
On the terrace of my old riots
I watch the river of the street flow
I shut my door to the commotion
(The moment finishing the vague landscape of memory)
And I drink my beer quietly
In the May twilight of Paris on the Seine.

The last fiber of my belonging
Is ripped away by the kora player...

to my double

In a low voice you who judge me and who sound this same deaf
    cry like the voice of blood

You in the foliage of midnight who write down the number of
    the cross
And who no longer wants to know
In a low voice you who growl in the foam and who puff in the
    voice of the Terral when it lowers its voice

Look I come with bare hands my heart scarcely veiled
And I bring you my millennia of history
This guilty history spattered with blood sperm and pus

Now it's time to explain to the witness what lying is
When the great South wind has swept all memory away.

To Maurice Merllié

It's December and the herds down there go South
Amid the stumps and loose white stones.

Enough of migrations and enough of transhumances!
I no longer want to break in the winds
that pass through the South
In the heavy rains washing the ossuaries of childhood
Imported at present by the camouflaged lookouts of my
  constellations
They'll no longer recognize me.

Far from the breathing sea
The road to the future cast as a bridge
On a space so dizzying
On such an absence

Nothing to declare to the customs of the past!

Msasani Bay

Pass. So who would want to stop the wave crested with foam and wind on this Msasani morning? The sharks cruise beyond the lagoon, death in the coral orchards...

Hand high on the polystyrene bulrush—ballad of the long-legged bait, poor poor Dylan!* Spool! The thread spools when the barracuda strikes, breaking the masturbatory surge.

Lily turns over, her blue bathing suit running along her crotch.

And the water that sculpts the vagina offered under the annoying fabric.

---

* The phrase "ballad of the long-legged bait," after the title of the poem by Dylan Thomas, is in English in the original. Fanchette also writes the words "spool" and "spools" in English.

THE SURVIVORS

to Sinclair Beiles

Will the bad autumn again throw you
Onto the brittle paths of wandering?
The black bird your landscape
The dead tree and the iced-over pond

Will the black rider of unhappiness pass by
To get lost in the thick of the fog?
Will the blind bird fall
On the black rustling rotting earth?

Your name gets lost like the number of a lost dream
Yet you still walk upright amid the ruins
Of a world that no longer deserves to survive.

for some Red Riding Hood
lost at my house in winter...

Rather than roses of winter
The thin flames in the hearth
Javelins to pierce the frozen heart
And the fingers harder than the flint shards
To scratch the glass of the offered skin

Rather than disaffected words
The wolf's gaze in the gloom of silence.

to René Coutel

This moment like hyacinth in February
Like a woodpecker in the hammering forest

I'd seen it shadow at the end of the trail
Behind the bed of massacred leaves
I'd seen this moment pensive
At the edge of the frozen pond

This morning the dogs that give
And the triumphal salvos of the horns

And the deer that travels
In the eternity of its death.

to Claude Vigée

That one who struggles in the obscure under the breathing skin
and who doesn't yet have a name
That one who sails against the rapids of dizziness
on the back of the eyelids
and who will burst into the day it invents

That one who opaque cancels anguish
in the very place of anguish
and who is finally born to his *name*

in the fragile transparency of morning.

CRUISE

To Edwin Mullins

The bird of carnage turns in the surprise of its own dizziness.
After is already begun and the mornings of childhood quiet
    down waves upon waves.

I go around the world and I go around life
Between two puffs of this ship that goes like destiny toward a
    fabulous Africa
Where the grenade in the blaze of the leaves
Bursts like segmented memory.

From here the sky is earth in its roadbed
The sea is only the sea pounding between the walls of the
    horizon
The forge breathing the fugue of breath
And the predatory seagull announces only the purpose of the
    earth

After was already begun in the disorder of the Azorean lavas

In the empty boiling of expectation
And the day was snapping like a bamboo stick
And was wounding the hand that wanted to grab it.

Coming from the sea we're the Greeks of Negritude
The Pascuans of the improbable.

Behold restored
The sea of lava the black sparkles of the obsidian
The stone daisy up there on Tenerife...
All this space all this time too vast for our desire.

And the ocean that pounds here unique and unchangeable
Between the parentheses of the moment
Here and now.

DISSENT ISLAND

to the memory of Pierre Renaud

The green night of the South had tamed nothing
The island burst forth with the vehemence of race
Once again blood encroaches on the low tides.
Memory, remind me of the name of this voyage
Back to the land of too-much-childhood
I've denied nothing of my share of light.
And now the island returns to its place
In the triumphal procession of the first day.

Yesterday even so.
I thought I saw death in the blue eye of a sea urchin.

(Poste Lafayette, Mauritius, August 31, 1977)

The Visitation of the Plover Bird

(1980)

to René Major

The Visitation of the Plover Bird

Tall grasses,
Transhumant herd of tall grasses
As soon as it was in the fault of the plural wind
Memory lit up.

Down there in the tied-up forest,
The venemous ambush,
My eyes opened to the miraculous birth.

This door that opens and that represses
A whole history of absence and refusal
This door that erases the night
And
The sea always to deafen
The litanies of fire and desire
To cancel absence.

It was down there in this country
of the always watched sixth sense
from the top of the lookouts of memory
Burning in the fire of the same absence.
The lianas of the nighttime forest
clutched desire and
defeated even its name.
It was the time of our limbo:
blood's surrender beat there.

The visitation on the eighth day
of the plover bird
called with the telepathy of solitude
tells me the double allegiance.
Again.
The triangle of the tern crosses
an ancient history.
The mythology of the islands beats there,
reaches the other side of reason.
I know every word whispered
by this foam liturgy
to the neat fissure of the past
like lava bursting.

I know every gesture of this tree
that dodges the wind
and the bitonal song of the bird of the lands
hanging on the clusters of the lilacs.

Everything breaks against the reef-screen of the South.
The South is my downstream my upstream
my lucky star the end of my sure course.

Departure was the secret code of this childhood.
So many ruins lifted in the memory of the saxifrage
in the arrested gesture the mass interrupted.
In deep sea October the ship becomes an island.
An immense water lily unfolds in my head
A happy tumor.

The opera for a moment stiffened
opening the constant clearing
in the distance of the time that is space.
The snake of the weeks the months the years
starts dancing
under the forgetful flute of the present.

Once again making its way along the crest line
Once again the morning beheaded
And the roastery of the capital city.

My street and its rumor in the palms of anguish
the gray wall of winter the cobblestones paving
the zone of difficult habit:
My divided territory.

Low sky equalizer for the swallow of the eternal return
Beyond these swamps where the lead of the winter sky flows
Way down South
A star in danger calls for help
On the other side of the light-years.

I remember the fragments of a massacre.

Your life?
Think of the boat striking in the sargassos
the threatened light running in the liana-filled forest
on this island lifted in the dawn of Msasani.

The mask inside the head of shadow
gives you a mocking look
And the time that drinks its eyes
the time of a flash in the prison of the eyelashes:
It's called desire
And it's strong enough to push away
all the door panels of the night.
It's called death.
The knife blow in the nerves of the moorings.

What else am I than this remorse at being myself
This crumpled memory of an unfinished dream?
And this lost voice that speaks through my voice
What does it say except the course of an absence?

Once again the lichen tatooed on the rock
Once again this bird hanging on dizziness
Somewhere the landscape has collapsed
I no longer know the name of the painter
or these colors.

The Gillette-blue sky
over the dust cloud of the heath
and in the fleeting trace
maybe without memory
the foreseen gaping of the sea.

Mahler's cavalry
reaping the dense grass of this heath
Here in the land of West Penwyth
And the day that travels winding in the summer.

Standing on the inner belvederes
in the sudden clamors of silence
I know I deserved the Sea
that will never be tamed
this hunger abiding
from this boat-world
suspended over the sea.

I travel in the bright freedom
of the words of childhood:
the privet and the mango tree
the sea and the bird in the wind.
And you anchored in the solid layer
Carved (carving) in the destiny of the rock
Caught in the very core
Figured (figuring) by/in the definitive scene.

And this is how *sketch* resembles *stress*
on the glyphless page of the book I'm reading.

The lamp always spills a parsimonious
ray into the dark sand.
I strike a tree like a match
and I flood the night farthest away
from its moving rings.

Wild midnight stamping
like the horses in westerns
in the corral under attack.

From this blockage in the landscape shattered yesterday
From this hard ridge of forgotten basalt
Swarm the bees of light
With sticky wings.

Who speaks to whom here?
Which word threatened by the gag of shadow?
Starry the mirror
Clamors have refracted toward the shadow mouth.
Absence that whistles between the teeth
Forgetfulness where the body capsizes

Ruins.

Maybe that happened on the steps of those forgotten countries whose airplanes delimit the traces written in the cultivated lands of Vexin-en-France; maybe that happened in the deserts of Ethiopia that I was traveling through last summer...

The beating of life; the wells where, in the evening, nubile girls carrying amphoras lingered and laughed while munching on leaves whose red juice they spat out (rules from on high for these willing virgins accountable for the blood of first penetration).

It was a whole possibility of stories in the time that's no longer time, when the hand of mankind and the telluric disruptions dislocated visible time...

Here, lying in the Beauce summer, like yesterday on the edge of the nighttime marlpit, I think of you, perverse virgin, Romanesque virgin with a boy's torso, with a clean cut inflicted by the ploughshare above those hips that desire arranged to the motion of the abolished sea.

Under the sticky salty rain
in the forcing house of the equinox-island
he walks as far as the crown of basalt
of the Wols under their abstract lichens.
Always in place is the giant mango tree
that reserves among its outcropping roots
a few kinds of slender sarcophagi
where the bodies of lovers have lain
and tamed the lush grass.

Noon sets aside the braids of rain.
The *bulbul* sings a quenched happiness
and strikes the dozen blows of haughty solitude.

That happens somewhere in the world that belongs to us.
All it takes is to knock over the censer of memory and its
    threatened embers.
Absence doesn't close off any landscape.

The grass that waves in the wind
The time that hits its stride
In the riddle of the cloud.
I drink the light of water
on the pebbles
Alert to the breath of the world's arteries
Communing to the fiery word
Pierced by lightning.

POEM IN NOVEMBER

to Martine

I

It will be in the time of here or there,
The wind driven out of the slivers of silence.
A bird will row in the vengeful space
Heavy in the sun
The time of the oblique shadow under the sundial.
The hourglass run out in the obscure of the dream,
The skein of light unwound to bind the time
from here and there.
When the rose of fire and the crystal of the ice
Will be a single imprint
A trace on the rock of the world disappeared
A lichen tatooed on the void of time
The October smoke on the Romanesque chapel
unwinding in the softness of the trees
And the fallow that runs in the South-facing perspective
Bring back the Crémats mountain, the pyres of piety
There on the Southern island, the clawed alignment of the
    aloes:
Here softness of autumn, there violent softness
Under the sun-hammered granite awning.

II

It's taken me all this time to realize that there's no exile
That exile is the dislocation between the time that's no longer
    time
and the place that's no longer place.
I'm standing in the murky light
Fastened to little things, a smell, a color…
The smell of the sea breeze crosses the salty space of the lagoon
that lives in me,
that beats in my hemisphere-roaming blood.
A thousand distinct colors, tender blue here,
Hammering of light there,
Come to me at the same time.
I live on the pallet of an insane God who thinks he's an artist.
Being from here and from there has taught me my own opacity
and my own transparency.
I'm the one to name and cross this space,
I'm the one to build this bridge over the time that's mine.

I'm *here* in my waking verticality
One,
Compact, fragile, and infrangible.

III

Within myself from the nameless people from the cleavages,
These two movements coexist
Summarized by the scathing anger of aloe and the leaf
that glides in the reddish light.
A landscape slipping from memory turns in the wheel of the
seasons.
Broken crystals serve as landmarks there.
I'm not from here. I'm no longer from elsewhere.
I sink into the verticality of my body.
I coil into the horizontality of my years.
Above me flies unmoving the bird called Absence.
I no longer walk in the hollowness, the vacant
Where the echo of my footsteps resounds like a salvo.

THE ADVENTURE OF THE POEM

to Michel Deguy and Pierre Oster

I

Of violent death
The poem will die at the edge of the poem.
Regiment my heart to the outposts.
There won't be a rarer plant
The very argument of radium.

A season of lightning advances
To disintegrate mankind.
A whole season of lightning
For the pride of being a man.

And what a mess of words
Blind and staggering in the preface!
Further, the lie,
The astonishment whistled by vowels
And the despair of having
Given language no alibi.

Silent is the night to the shipwreck watch.
Regiment my sentinel heart.
Throw it in the wheels
Of perpetual motion.
Children's voices in the twilight
Bait memory.
But all words have died of windy death
Between algebra and the poem.

II

As long as the night moves,
The poem stops,
Ship fires standing, on the high sea.
The Southern Cross has toppled,
All the winds cast off.
They'll harvest the shipwrecks
And the shout will stay ellipsis.

The poem is in phase lag,
It has missed all the trains in all the stations.
Time won't be diagrammed.

Ophelia has drowned under the willow—
So many snows since then on Elsinore!
The aging Magi
No longer hope for the Star.
The moon has sold its legend
And the dreamy earth has broken its moorings.

I'd like to *say*.
Everything's left to say on this ageless earth
Who will recover the keys to the dead language,
The light that's flowed to the secrets of the stained glass?
Who will reinvent the first equation?
Of the verb and the sun?

III

Between the moment and the poem
In the greatest confusion of light-years
Is written the staggering adventure of language,
The time of the impossible possible.

I say "larch"
And forests move with branches
Through secrets of coal and iron
Adrift since the first equation of the world.
I'd like to say larch
The sure adventure of the whispering sap
Under the night of the bark.

But the moment escapes.
We collide with the bars of the shout
And the lightning in our hands fades out.
We're too far and too near
The world's pulsation.

The trip was without history.
Constellations gushed in the morning
Behind the yards
And the poem shattered into foam lace.
Travelers we had made our own
The full breathing and at times the sweat of words.
We had shattered into crystals
The underground veins of language.
We've been fooled by the poem.

For the poem has condemned itself to death.
The poem has betrayed emotion,
Emotion has betrayed memory.
The poem had no history
Like the oblique time of the shadow under the leaves.
It's enough for me to say "wind"
To betray the cyclones.
I say "water" for high death,
I spell "river"
But what do I know about the childhood of fountains?

Like the order of mornings
The poem resurfaces from the underground river
Where all memory gets lost.
I'll be the rower of the verb.
I'll sail up the poem.

IV

Landscapes die of departure
Inside the scripts of a windy night
And the key to the faces rusts,
Forgotten on some vacant lot.

The mills of the word
Have nothing left to bite into
And the poem got shipwrecked
In the four corners of writing.

I'll keep quiet. And my silence
Will linger as something
Infinitely fragile, infinitely patient
A hint of what remains to be said.

And maybe someday, tagged with its own light,
To a child who will have learned nothing
Except the Gospel of the seedful land
And the hoped-for pilgrammage of sources toward the sea,
The world will be royally given back,
The recovered key to the faces,
The secret of landscapes in motion
From the other slope of the heart.

Memory of the Saxifrage

(Poems rediscovered: 1956–1991)

"We're born to bear time,
not to remove ourselves from it."
Jean-Paul de Dadelsen

Places; Commonplaces; Nonplaces

1   Roubignac

Will the wolf again turn into the October barn?
Now is here, on this Southern combe
Where the wine reddens on the still stiff vine
Here is now in the disaffected Romanesque
Chapel, windy at summer's end.
Heralding, devastating
The vacant time, in the vacant time.

2   Octon

to Brigitte and Jacques Temple

Spurges, asclepias with feathery pappi, laburnums.
Thorny breath
of rosemary; bumpy, light mauve tufts of April thyme in Octon
reserving among themselves the gaps of shadow where some-
times a dog turd
gleams chalky and bleached like a bone. Stony countryside of
the other
side of the fault beyond that red breach in the dry torrent…

3   QUAI DE BOURBON

The river's skin hardly shivers under the fast flick of the wind.
From the other bank, a woman's laugh (shout?): lone transparency
in the opacity of the July night.

4   BAY OF MSASANI (TANZANIA)

From this offshore of time, lost as if in oceanic vastness,
to find back the island lying at the base of the island: the toil
of the coral,
the questioning of the light, and the alluvial song I no longer
name exile

5   The blue, a fish flying in the luminous haze of
summer. Far away,
But coiling in the spiral so as to return
Here.

6   GEORGETOWN (DC)
(musing on a painting by Andrew Wyeth)

The gaze of morning at grass level, with eyespots, gathering
the smell and the color, the oriole and the cricket, yesterday's
cold ember, the music of moribund Schubert—and my life in
tears...

7   AVENUE MOZART

All it takes is one rose in the tapered vase of Bohemian glass to light this room, to soften the light on the aged wood of the secretary,
to bring on an undefinable calm order, to furnish an undefinable peaceful happiness.
To travel here!

8   PARIS-UNHEIMLICH

to Serge Sabinus

Familiar and terrible like the nose in the middle of the face
Like the gray Metro and its gray ghosts at eleven o'clock at night in capital Paris
Terrible and familiar like Monday staggering at the edge of the week…
Capital letters of words suddenly forgotten at the pediment of things:
All is other
All is new
Oh! to be this other
To go out with it through the blind door of the wall
To come back in through the tain of the mirror
Opaque and transparent.

9   Seagull keeper of its own gestures
Crosser of abolished space
That yesterday I called "desire."

10   Salagou

                                        to Katioucha Pillet

Two sigillated vases amid the ocher glitters in the churned sand
and a broken sword restored by the ancient manor here evoke
a bimillennial gesture. Today the dam water threatens the rem-
nants and the Spanish broom bushes float like water hyacinths
or carnivorous algae.

The old tower of Roques that I recently explored on the mound
off the road to Celles and the woodwork of the ruffe soil have
been leveled and the water whirls ten fathoms deep. I walk
without memory in the shifting light. My landscapes contra-
dict each other. I'll have learned to live here as if my roots had
traveled to this ungrateful land, this rocky red ground. Hence
saxifrages…

11   January in Vaucluse

The ocher earth motionless under the path of the cloud. At the
bottom, the white
stones and the parasols touched by green sunlight. It's January
in Vaucluse.
The heavy-hearted winter holds its breath. A buzzard perched

on a hedge
that separates us from the highway embankment watches the
gliders climb
the luminous heights of the sky.
This terrible desire to live suddenly! It's the same force that in
two months will unlock the black bark, the imprisoned fruit.

12   COLLIOURE

to the memory of Valérie de Carpelan

She who,
She who comes walking under the green glow of the lighthouse,
Scattering the nighttime sand;

She who,
She who, lost voice, ancient voice,
Melts into the ever renewed
Voice of the sea pounding this Catalan inlet,

There etched her laugh and her harmonic basses...

YESTERDAY THE SEA...

to Issa Asgarally

Calm. The sea stretching far away
Cradles the sky of the exiles.
The foam is loyal to the spray.
I deny the soul of the isles.

King, I have lost my caravels,
I have let green-haired childhood flee.
I swim alongside the small eels
Against the currents of the sea.

King, I have sold my bittersweet
Heritage for other kingdoms
And hostage to my only fate
I clutch emptiness in my palms.

Calm. The sea stretching far away
Cradles the sky of the exiled.
The foam is loyal to the spray.
What russet suns burn my eyelid?

(February 29, 1956)

MEMORY

to Philippe Rey

Twenty-seven years. And only invented
these thickets of memory where age gets wounded
Anguish surpassed before the purest crystal of death
I inquire and it's the fragile death of sands
that seedfully answers the nameless husk.

Crossed rejected the sure shelter of sighs
time casts ashes on this bit of memory
in tune with our hands.
The fact remains that at the edge of day you have invoked
the wind that was clearing its path in the roll of wheat
grown in water that no baptism had wounded.
But where to invent this fragile place in exile of snow
when the wind has blurred our most secret geographies?

Yet,
may this bit of happiness move among the lianas
of the native forest with deaf blazes
the sure path of blood irrigates its sleep
and dying he reaches its only dwelling.

(1957)

River

There, on its fallow belly, in the brief time of words,
The whole sky upside down moves through the lianas.
My hand slips into travel and wakes a crystal.
From the source time has captured the estuary.

River of scattered rumor, of goldsmith's games
To what ripe season do I at last spell out,
Fragile, whispered as close as can be to the lips
The only day of rock as the dream runs out?

Reaching the sea I learn the horizon alone.
The fog disperses on the eyelashes' heath.
A wandering sun takes root in the virgin fields.
And the world's kernel puts my exile to seed.

(October 30, 1958)

for Frédérique

Never have I been nearer the silken edge of tears.
I say Frédérique. Vowels of joy light up
The tender green of the landscape. The sky arms itself
With the thin javelins of the light. The salt and the foam
In the hands of a lingering Magus become eternal.

Paradise lost starts again beyond the Seventh Fountain.

My February lily of the valley, from this season risen early
Against the night, I think your name, its vowels eaten by wind
And the May of words bursts on the blank page,
My child who teaches me standing on the slope of my age
More than the flower, the secret summer of fruit and the seeded,
sleepy harvests.

From a twilight the tattooed sky still weighs on the tears.
The wind has turned; its emeralds lit up
At the first sunlight squeezed in the fallow dawn.
Silence of water. A golden fish gets caught in the foam's net.

Here's the evening opening onto the salt of the reefs
And the only crack in the voice of the Terral,
Suddenly the music of the source on the plainsong of the estuary.

(February 28, 1959)

FROM THE SEA

to my brother Régis

I

Every parting is painful to the memory of those men
From the sea who got lost amid the lianas of their footsteps
In a birdless city in the dirty snows of exile.
The cloak of hard wind still burns the salt of their faces
And in their eyes ships smash the order of the archipelagos.
Every parting is painful. Foam and wave sculpture
And white drift of sails under the very heavy patterns of the sky.

Metamorphosis in the sea daylight, the swarms of light rustle;
The homebound ships cruise the open sea of happy memory
And the flowers of shadow open to the orchards of the sleepy sea.
The sea. And its braids unfurling before the fine gold of our gazes
And the stars unmoored, one Southern night, amid the yards.

II

The sails of the windmill learn silence on the millrace of dark water;
Memory would like, lightly drawn, rare gestures,
Shadowy gestures of swimmers on the sealed coral grounds.
Here the architecture is in the order of frost and its rosaces;
There the wind carves the rock into the shape of prone corpses
And the paths of burned grass shatter with the assault of the hills.
It's not so much exile as it is contempt for the female earth,
For the shifting and treacherous residue of the debacle of basalts!
Their earth pregnant with sobs whose wounds the sea reopens
Launches its salvos of violence in the sooty sky of Europe;
And the only Magi they love are those of the starless return.

III

Sea, absence of sea begins after the last boulevard
Of this ossuary-city.
The frescos of fog fade into the night that's no longer time.
But this dawn a ship sets sail on the calm waters of sleep,
A ship rigged with wind carrying the birds of return.

IV

Earth. From here the earth is the hill on the horizon of dawn.
The Southern constellations sleep on the lagoons of dead water.
From an ancient season drifting leaves bring them
The salvation of the raucous earth that their roots got caught in:
Emeralds of the virgin morning and the fallow sky of bracken.
And to guide them in the channel, amid the traveling algae
A hanging seagull white banner in the earth wind;

And then this was a holiday song of the black dock of foresails.
And this was a song as at the long-long-ago parting.
But the only Magi they love are those of the giftless return.

V

Morning on the City saw men cry who had
Wandered to the end of the night, lost up to the salt of their tears.

(June 1959)

POSTCARD

to Danièle Saint-Bois

The cemeteries in Brittany are open at night.
The sea everywhere is open at night.
At Douarnenez the cemetery advanced into the night and onto
    the sea.

To Marie-Claude running away on the road to Brest
To Marie-Claude putting her thumb up to death on the road to
    Brest
To Marie-Claude sitting in the acrid scent of the grass on the
    side of the road
To Marie-Claude whom I've never seen
I make the offering of these flowers of dust
Pulled out of the grass along the road
On the anonymous mound in the Douarnenez cemetery.

And the sea rolled toward the sandbar
And the night rolled and wept to the open sea,
Toward Ushant.

(1976)

My Vigilance

to Valérie

I loved you You were the morning caught in our giddiness
And you were the evening of sayable promises
The night surrounding the high fortresses of the wind
You were the scorched earth where the grass was growing again.

No wave put out our two-way lights on the sea.

Since then I relentlessly muse that you and I
        will die far from each other.

(1961)

Novel

to Domenica von F.

Afterward,
>   when the first lineament of lying takes shape,
>   which she knows won't fill in the breach in devoured time;

Afterward,
>   when in the lustral shower in fact intended to wash away the
>   drool
>   and the stickiness of what she calls "love";

All right,
>   may come to her lips a Verdi aria or the poignancy of one of the
>   "last lieder";

All right,
>   may be solved the riddle of Wols's etching blessing her bed;

Well,
>   surveyors of emptiness, we take measure of the desert
>   or else huskies with painted muzzles, warriors returned from
>   everything,
>   we again crawl up the ice floe...
>   Millennia later,
>   I dream of the perfect winter of our wars, of her geometries of
>   frost, of the sharpness of her bite,

Of the stony bird of carnage.

(March 3, 1991)

Equitable Exile
Michel Deguy
Translated by Hassan Melehy

The poem begins with *Osmoses*, in meter. It's romantic: classical. "My soul is this, my soul is that"; "One day I would say..." Later on, it comes back to itself; it's "the adventure of the poem" (pp. 161–65).

Lyrical the tone will remain. Here the "I" learns itself, inscribes itself, forms itself—proscribes itself as far as this admirable maxim: "What else am I than this remorse at being myself?" (p. 150). It sought its *destination*—as the final opening page of February 28, 1992, tells us (p. 19)—by gauging itself against its wake, in keeping with the backward motion ("back to the land of too-much-childhood," p. 141) of the exile who also knows he is "a bearer of the sign" (p. 19).

The poems are oriented to the Island, this "world-ship," this "seed, almond [*amande*]," the verbal adjective of love [*amour*]. The poems are dedicated—to brothers, women, daughters, friends. Jean's fabric was that of the faithful: exile tempers faithfulness. Until the end—Ithaca was at both ends of the modern fragmentary odyssey. Alternately his Elba and his Saint Helena.

The Island is called *Equinox*. What are the halves that the Island evenly divides? What is the division of this poet? Land between two seas, the island; sea or sky between two lands, the voyage; and pulling apart or joining together the two interchangeable hemispheres, the unsuperimposable North and South; and the two great languages of the bilingual person, and his "share of Negritude" (p. 51), and his share of candor; and "two lives" (p. 28) torn apart, being alone and being two, and to his double and to his half. And one part of him was a scientist through analysis and the other a poet through poetry.

The Island is his former island: ex-isle. And he is that singular person, of denial (p. 174) in this denial of denial (p. 141): "I've denied nothing…") turning and returning in this provisional identity: exile.

Jean was voluble and multiple, verb, active and passive voice, "figured (figuring) by/in the definitive scene" (p. 153)—in which we understand from this professional of psychoanalytic terms a site other than that of the primal scene. For his poem is discreet; Orpheus (*membra disjecta*) appears in pieces, is concealed in fragments. The drama of his life hides: a secret communication to his addressees, in which the torment quiets down.

What is exile? I once dreamed of crafting a poem from the *table of contents* of a collection (and I did it in *Jumelages*). If I thought I could do it here (it's impossible), a collection of the collection, with its own contents made of mango and larch, saxifrage and hills, bitterness and passion, clover and plover (his poetic ear, following his analytical ear, gives us a word, *pluvier* in French, filled with *pluie*, rain, and *vieillir*, to age), I would bring together, for this table of contents as poem, the maxims where the *here* balances out the *there*, and those of the Magi who arrive as they age (p. 45) and return starless (p. 178).

Who has thought of the Magi's voyage of return? And maybe of their second departure, like that of Ulysses before the underworld? It's the round trip that makes the poem, and this second age that returns to the steps of childhood recovered as now lost forever.

First, there's the geographic liberation from the here and the there, which become each other through exile and return, which are related to, are transferred to, and reciprocate each other: the division between the "hummingbird in the mango tree" and the "oriole in the cherry tree" (p. 28)—a very discreet quotation of René Char, from whom Jean Fanchette tells us he received the sign (p. 19); "two lives" torn apart (p. 28). Then there's the here of the poem. The poem makes and becomes the place: a gift of ubiquity. And readers, following him everywhere, might not know where they are. Finally, what counts is the in-both-directions, the acquired equivocality, multivocality, and polysemy, the reversal of the relation (the turning and re-turning of his course) in which the relation is learned as more essential than the terms it sets forth; the reversion and the retroversion—compa-ss-rison. Exile is "the exile of the world" (p. 105).

Poetry, deferring and transferring, is always circumstantial: in the here that it now prefers and where its poem carries out its affairs—afferent, efferent—at the same time it opens another there than the faraway that one sees from here, a further-beyond than the background of the locality it speaks from, another vista than the one we have before our eyes, on our back, "under our hand," another circumstance than *this one*: displacing, canceling, piercing its current locale so as to confer *another*, of the other—very elsewhere, very near.

So at this moment, at this same time, itself, the lyric "I," this relater of the relation, conducts an *orchestra of the world* at that moment that doesn't exist, but it is *as though it made it play.* For such is the operation (the grace) that exile, with no guarantee, makes possible and favorable.

Goodbye, Jean.

Michel Deguy

I'm Not from Here,
I'm No Longer from Elsewhere
J. M. G. Le Clézio

TRANSLATED BY HASSAN MELEHY

*E*quinox Island is a particularly moving collection in Jean Fanchette's œuvre. Moving because it imperiously recalls another poet of exile and belonging, Arthur Rimbaud. The two men have something in common. First, travel. Rimbaud, at his life's midpoint, after he'd stopped writing, went to live in Malta and Egypt, then the Harrar region, and returned to die in France, of cancer, at age forty. And the ship, the *Amazone*, on which he was repatriated, when he was already dying, was one of the liners of the Compagnie Générale Maritime that ran the service between the Indian Ocean (Aden) and Marseille, and also carried passengers from Mauritius.

Fanchette lived Rimbaud's experience, but in reverse. Rimbaud entered poetry, raised up the French language, transformed it forever. Then he went silent, and he traveled to the Indian Ocean. Fanchette went in the opposite direction because he began by traveling, leaving Mauritius; instead of moving east he went west. He went to Europe, and there he found poetry, theater (his engagement with Jacob Moreno's adventure in psychodrama is well known), and at the same time he practiced his profession as a psychiatric doctor. His voyage passed from silence (Mauritius, in a certain way the island of silence) to the illumination of poetry, and then it was interrupted by death. There's something strange in this correspondence.

I believe both of them may be considered adventurers in every sense of the word: the adventure of poetry but also the adventure of life. And this extreme experience, this experience of poetry and travel, is the terrain where the two poets meet.

But they meet especially in the value of words. Fanchette and Rimbaud are both poets who demand much from vocabulary, from language. They're poets who have no truck with ornament. They're in exactness. For them, poetry is an absolute of the human quest. With one as with the other is a necessity to access the real—not the real of the everyday, but the real hidden in the heart of things, the dazzle, the sensorial charge, the kinesthetic truth. With one as with the other, the same freedom. There are very surprising encounters. In a poem, his first great poem, "The Drunken Boat," Rimbaud speaks of "peninsulas unmoored [*péninsules démarrées*]." In *Equinox Island*, Fanchette spontaneously uses the same image: he writes "stars unmoored [*étoiles démarrées*]" ("From the Sea," p. 178). The same ship, the same voyage, the same sounds of wind in the yards, the sound that he imagines and that has transcended the poetry of Rimbaud, that invited him to the voyage. It's the taste for the sea, this taste for adventure that one finds again in the poetry of Fanchette. His desire for the elsewhere, for the new, his need for truth.

The other meeting point between these two poets is what I'll term the "memory of youth." When we speak of memory, in general we think of someone older, near life's end. "I shall not write memories," proclaims Lautréamont, completely in his rebellion against (God) the father. For Fanchette, as for Rimbaud, memory is that of youth, a memory based not on the wisdom of experience but the flashing intuition of childhood. We can't help thinking of the definition Rabintranath Tagore provides in *Fireflies*:

> The child ever dwells in the mystery of ageless time,
> unobscured by the dust of history.

There's something naïve, innocent, childlike in Fanchette's approach, as there is in Rimbaud. There's also the extraordinary appetite for life, the taste for sensations tied to childhood that one finds in Fanchette's great poems, such as "The Noons of Blood" or "Osmoses."

Let's listen to "The Poem of the Child Tree":

The rhythmic pulses of a landscape
Vibrating in the veins of the tree,
The brother rock and his omens
Were grasped in the morning
Brought to me from the depth of ages.
[...]
The tree remembers the seed,
The slow night of roots,
The forests of resin and shade,
Until the call of the first bird
Across centuries of waiting.

And I, the child of one second,
Amid the flowing gold of the broom bushes,
I watch over that moment set down
By the anguish of millions of years
In the world's bright disorder.
      (pp. 27–28)

This is the appetite for life, the appetite for sensations. In Fanchette's work there is the taste for precise resonance. The magic of the world isn't something acquired. For Fanchette, it's a certainty that he received in childhood, that guided him through his life, as prescience. We've often spoken—evoking Fanchette—of exile. He himself spoke of his "exile": he defined himself as a poet of transplant, a poet of departure. But this mix of sensations, leading as far as anatopism, is his force of resistance in exile, the inner truth that permeates him, the childhood memory that forever pursued him, that assailed and obsessed him. Mauritius is the "back country" of his poems, as he calls it. In everything he wrote, Mauritius is present. Not in nostalgia or fleeting memories but as current and physical individuality, made entirely of sensations—a real life, more real than the material reality he found in London or Paris.

We've listened to the poem of the tree, the poem of the mixture of trees. Trees know no borders. They grow freely wherever the wind blows their seeds, wherever human beings root them. They can't be identified with a place. Likewise, the range of sensations doesn't amount to an identity. Or else it will be a provisional identity, an evolving, moving identity.

When Jean Fanchette came to Paris, he bore a message. Could it have been the message that Jean Paulhan never heard, the message that Malcolm de Chazal sent him and that remained a dead letter? The relationship between Chazal the mystic and Fanchette the instinctive isn't at first sight obvious. If it's likely that they crossed paths—even if only at the crossroads of *La Louise*, where nothing that moved around in Mauritius between the heights and Port Louis failed to turn up—their mutual strangeness is quickly apparent. And yet there's a coincidence.

Chazal's writings were received, celebrated, and listened to in Paris, even if the writer never attempted the pilgrimage. But his deep word— which in him was deeply Mauritian, meaning full of sensations and convictions attached to his island—was poorly understood, even disdained. That's why Paulhan later broke with Chazal. It wasn't a betrayal but a misunderstanding, the worst kind and the most irreparable of breaches.

In a way Fanchette managed to bear and restore that word—because, unlike Chazal, Fanchette is a fairly modest creator. He's a poet who proclaims nothing definitively, who states no diktat but instead asks questions. He questions himself, he questions us, he proposes a vivid music, a youthful music, with a Rimbaudian accent, not at all in time with the thundrous music sometimes heard in Paris from an inhabitant of a distant island. The first truth that must be stated is that neither Chazal nor Fanchette are writers of exoticism. Quite the contrary: they oppose that counterfeit, that decoy. What they say is marked by insularity, by the splitting that people from the islands know. But they don't use it as backdrop or dress-up. In a way they're stripped of it, because for them honor lies in that discomfort. If we sense condemnation in them—lofty for Chazal, fragile for Fanchette—it subsists in the affirmation of their truth, without detour or compromise.

There's a poem that speaks of just that, "Presto Vivace":

> I'm always on the run I've never stopped
> All done while running love and birth and death
> I chase down suns I've never even seen
> I run after dreams I'll no longer have
>
> I catch the seasons in their endless cycle
> of dazzling green, of metamorphoses
> Time's not for me I keep watch on the clouds
> Drifting behind them toward vague silences
>
> A nameless meteor in the sky of ages
> No longer even knowing the place I fled
> in outer space I lead a hellish whirl
> Of jeering phantoms who have never died.
>> (p. 25)

In the foreword to *Equinox Island*, which he wrote in 1992, he says:

> I've always written poems. Poetry has been the testimony to my most constant fidelity to the unsayable, an unconscious and ferocious struggle, and at the same time a destination rather than a destiny. [...]
>
> The back country of these poems is naturally

the island of my childhood: Mauritius, its salvos
that won't stop reverberating in the echoes of exile,
those deaf blazes in memory.
>
> (p. 19)

Exile can't be political exile. Nor can it be economic exile. It's the need that Fanchette had—at a certain time in his life, which corresponds to the time in one's existence when one must face up to the world—to leave and become another. Exile is a breach deep inside oneself, which may be identified only by those of uncertain origin and incomprehensible destination:

> It's taken me all this time to realize that there's no exile
> That exile is the dislocation between the time that's no
>> longer time
> and the place that's no longer place.
> I'm standing in the murky light
> Fastened to little things, a smell, a color...
> The smell of the sea breeze crosses the salty space of the
>> lagoon
> that lives in me,
> that beats in my hemisphere-roaming blood.
> [...]
> I'm *here* in my waking verticality
> One,
> Compact, fragile, and infrangible.
>> ("Poem in November," II, p. 159)

And a little further:

> I'm not from here. I'm no longer from elsewhere.
> I sink into the verticality of my body.

I coil into the horizontality of my years.
Above me flies unmoving the bird called Absence.
I no longer walk in the hollowness, the vacant
Where the echo of my footsteps resounds like a salvo.
        ("Poem in November," III, p. 160)

"I'm not from here. I'm no longer from elsewhere." Truly this is the secret that touches us in Fanchette's work: this discomfort. Human beings properly belong nowhere because they're from everywhere. Their country is movement, what carries them toward other human beings. The line familiar to islanders that the Greeks called *horizein* (that which limits) doesn't confine the poet, but rather calls him to other places, toward his other self. Doesn't the Creole proverb say *lizié pena balizaze*, the eyes have no border, and don't the Tuaregs of the desert (islanders in their own way) affirm that their true country is the horizon?

Fanchette felt close to Africa. He made the trip to Tanzania—the coast of Mozambique where the soul of Mauritius was enclosed, its cursed part, forged in the slave camps of Zanzibar or Qiloa—and there he received one of the most beautiful poems ever written about slavery. It's called "From the Sea."

Every parting is painful to the memory of those men
From the sea who got lost amid the lianas of their footsteps
In a birdless city in the dirty snows of exile.
The cloak of hard wind still burns the salt of their faces
And in their eyes ships smash the order of the archipelagos.
Every parting is painful. Foam and wave sculpture
And white drift of sails under the very heavy patterns of the sky.

Metamorphosis in the sea daylight, the swarms of light rustle;
The homebound ships cruise the open sea of happy memory
And the flowers of shadow open to the orchards of the sleepy sea.

The sea. And its braids unfurling before the fine gold of our gazes
And the stars unmoored, one Southern night, amid the yards.
    (p. 178)

And on the beach in Tanzania, he discovered the very violent image of slavery, the metaphor of a destroyed world, of a violated world.

Pass. So who would want to stop the wave crested with foam and
    wind on this Msasani morning? The sharks cruise beyond the
    lagoon, death in the coral orchards...
Hand high on the polystyrene bulrush—ballad of the long-legged bait,
    poor poor Dylan! Spool! The thread spools when the barracuda
    strikes, breaking the masturbatory surge.
Lily turns over, her blue bathing suit running along her crotch.
And the water that sculpts the vagina offered under the annoying
    fabric.
    ("Msasani Bay," p. 134)

The exile Fanchette speaks of is also the burn of Africa, the phrase "The summer will be as hoarse as anger's jab" ("Seasons," p. 70), which he wrote in 1957, well before the first great wars of destruction in modern Africa, before Biafra, before Congo. The break with History imbues the poet with a feeling of the provisional. Identity is provisional because reason proposes nothing definitive to us, and because all of us humans are the "Pascuans of the improbable" ("Cruise," p. 139): like the Easter Island statues of unknown origin that stare into the distance without knowing what they're staring at.

So Fanchette's poetry speaks of the necessity to see with precision what we're made of—to read in ourselves what questioning is, what conjecture is.

Among Fanchette's claims, curiously, is the aversion to travel— "Enough of migrations" he says:

It's December and the herds down there go South
Amid the stumps and loose white stones.

Enough of migrations and enough of transhumances!
I no longer want to break in the winds
that pass through the South
In the heavy rains washing the ossuaries of childhood
Imported at present by the camouflaged lookouts of my
        constellations
They'll no longer recognize me.

Far from the breathing sea
The road to the future cast as a bridge
On a space so dizzying
On such an absence

Nothing to declare to the customs of the past!
        (p. 133)

And another poem, a refusal of fixed identity, of peremptory affirmation, "Yesterday the Sea":

Calm. The sea stretching far away
Cradles the sky of the exiles.
The foam is loyal to the spray.
I renounce the soul of the isles.

King, I have lost my caravels,
I have let green-haired childhood flee.
I swim alongside the small eels
Against the currents of the sea.

King, I have sold my bittersweet
Heritage for other kingdoms
And hostage to my only fate
I clutch emptiness in my palms.

Calm. The sea stretching far away
Cradles the sky of the exiled.
The foam is loyal to the spray.
What russet suns burn my eyelid?
(p. 174)

So this is *Equinox Island.*

Read these poems! They're current events. What Fanchette says about Africa is still true today. His doubt about identity is something many of us feel, because today exile digs into us, and in our minds the provisional declares itself. The search for identity, Fanchette teaches us, isn't a simple matter of belonging to—or escaping—a nation. It's a matter of questioning ourselves as to what we are, of asking what constructs us. What keeps us alive? How will we accept others? What will we get from them? How will we know how to love them?

Jean Fanchette's word, sadly, was broken off too early, like Rimbaud's. His word remains in suspense. And maybe that's what is most moving as one reads his poems. There's exactly poetry's own questioning of itself, thought that remains incomplete, movement that knows no end, life that has no final destination—the questioning that Fanchette offers us of himself, of the world, the very sensual, sensory evocation of the world, and his refusal to participate in the grand ideas, the grand debates, his refusal of any compromise with the grand pseudohumanist themes (fashionable in his time), his refusal of exoticism and simplicity being his only true credo. He believed quite firmly in humanity, he was a great humanist, though he refused to use the common words, the familiar words, of humanism. He was also from the sea, and he had nothing else to share but the discomfort of wanderers.

Fanchette's poetry is demanding; it's authentic in each of its phrases, in the richness of its rhythm, in the value of its words. It's no accident that in the modern world, imbued with theory and deaf to certainties, this very ancient voice conveys all the complexity and originality of Mauritian culture, no accident that this voice gives us faith in poetry.

J. M. G. Le Clézio
Mauritius, November 2008

Bibliography of Jean Fanchette's Works

Poetry:

Gerbes de silence. Marches de France, 1952.

Osmoses. Presse à bras de Montéro, 1954.

Les midis du sang. Debresse, 1956. Prix Paul Valéry.

Archipels. Voyelles, 1958. Prix Fénéon.

Identité provisoire. Two Cities, 1965 (lithographs by Jean Hélion).

Je m'appelle sommeil. Two Cities, 1977 (original drawings Jean Bessil).

La visitation de l'oiseau pluvier. Revue *Po&sie*, 1977, and Two Cities,
    1982 (limited edition with four lithographs by Jean-Max Toubeau).

L'Île Équinoxe. Stock, 1993; rpt., Philippe Rey, 2009, 2016, and 2023.

Novel:

Alpha du Centaure. Buchet/Chastel, 1975. Prix de la Langue Française,
    Académie Française.

Critical works:

"French Poetry 1960." *International Literary Annual* nos. 1–2 (1961):
    154–66.

With Pierre Leyris. *Poèmes et proses de la folie de John Clare*. Mercure
    de France, 1969.

Psychodrame et théâtre moderne. Buchet/Chastel, 1971. Prix des
    Mascareignes.

"Le Miroir et le Biseau." Preface to *Cités intérieures* by Anaïs Nin.
    Stock, 1975.

Translation:

Joyce McDougall and Serge Lebovici. *Dialogue avec Sammy:
    Contribution à l'étude de la psychose infantile*. Payot, 1984.

Born on the Indian Ocean island of Mauritius, JEAN FANCHETTE (1932–92) was a psychiatrist, writer, and editor who spent his adult life in Paris. While still in medical school he won several French national poetry prizes. In 1959, with the support of Anaïs Nin, he founded the French-English bilingual review *Two Cities*, which featured the work of many future notables, including Michel Deguy, Lawrence Durrell, and Octavio Paz. Under the Two Cities imprint, Fanchette published *Minutes to Go* (1959), the first "cut-up" experiments of William Burroughs, Brion Gysin, Sinclair Beiles, and Gregory Corso. In his region of origin Fanchette is highly celebrated: every two years since 1992, the Jean Fanchette Prize has been awarded to a writer from the islands of Mauritius, Rodrigues, Réunion, Madagascar, the Comoros, and Seychelles.

Originally from New England, HASSAN MELEHY lived all over the USA before settling in North Carolina in 2004, where he lives with his wife, Dorothea Heitsch. His first poetry collection, *A Modest Apocalypse*, was published by Eyewear in 2017. In addition to his creative writing he has written three books of criticism, most recently *Kerouac: Language, Poetics, and Territory* (Bloomsbury, 2016). He has translated works of criticism, philosophy, and social science from French, including Jacques Rancière's *The Names of History* (University of Minnesota Press, 1994). He teaches at the University of North Carolina, Chapel Hill.

www.ingramcontent.com/pod-product-compliance
Lightning Source LLC
Chambersburg PA
CBHW031513120626
46545CB00005B/1865